AND GOD SPOKE

Reflections from a Journey of Faith

Margaret Lim

Copyright © 2022 Margaret Lim

All rights reserved.

Cover design by Margaret Lim

Book design by Margaret Lim

No part of this book can be reproduced in any form or by written, electronic or mechanical, including photocopying, recording, or by any information retrieval system without written permission in writing by the author.

Scripture taken from the Holy Bible, NEW INTERNATIONAL VERSION, NIV Copyright © 1973, 1978, 1984, 2011 by Biblica, Inc. Used by permission. All rights reserved worldwide unless otherwise stated.

Published by Margaret Lim, Bedfordshire

Printed by Book Printing UK www.bookprintinguk.com

Remus House, Coltsfoot Drive, Peterborough, PE2 9BF

Printed in Great Britain

Although every precaution has been taken in the preparation of this book, the publisher and author assume no responsibility for errors or omissions. Neither is any liability assumed for damages resulting from the use of information contained herein.

ISBN: 978-1-3999-4263-8

INTRODUCTION

Dear Reader,

I am a follower of Jesus Christ and my relationship with Him gives me joy and peace as I journey through life. Although my faith has not always been strong, I can say from the heart that God has never failed me since I gave my life to him at the age of seven. He is my Rock in times of trouble and a faithful friend who has never left me. His love is limitless and beyond understanding.

In recent years God has moved me to develop my musical abilities by writing songs which express His heart, often through Scripture. These have been used in both church and personal worship. Music has always been the primary means by which I express myself, and I find it a delight to share my faith in this way, knowing that it blesses others too.

It was during the lockdown in March 2020 that I first felt the Holy Spirit prompting me to begin writing. With all the uncertainty and fear caused by the Covid 19 pandemic I had a sense of urgency to share the good news of God's love. Some of my reflections explain this in more detail and how we can enter into a personal relationship with Him.

With more time to spend in prayer and bible study I found that God was speaking to me and revealing truths from His heart, which I needed to express in writing. After some consideration and prayer, I began a blog called 'Margie's Notes' in which I shared my thoughts with the aid of illustrations and scripture references. The blog posts included thoughts on parables, psalms and other bible passages as well as personal thoughts and 'pictures' from the Holy Spirit.

The Revd. Canon Nigel Washington suggested that I should use some of my blog posts to create a book, providing a more permanent and tangible record of the thoughts and revelations I had been given. It has taken me a while to complete this, but it is now with pleasure and joy that I present this book, 'And God Spoke'. This is not to say I am an expert or have succeeded in living out all the lessons in this book. We are all a 'work in progress; and learn something new every day.

In this little book you will find a series of reflections based on what I believe God has said to me in my times of prayer, reflection and everyday experiences. When you read it, my prayer and hope is that you will be blessed, encouraged and expectant to hear God speak to you, as you go about your daily life and personal walk with Him.

Margaret Lim

September 2022

FOREWORD

I have known Margaret Lim for many years and for the last 12 to 15 years specifically as a member of the congregation at St Mary Magdalene Church, Westoning, where I was the vicar. Margaret is what I would term 'an authentic Christian,' honest and true, faithful and quietly fervent, dependable and original, thoughtful, dutiful and loving. Quite special. Her faith is real and her desire to share her faith has gradually grown in recent years. Increasingly her God given insights are plain to see.

Initially I was pleased to encourage Margaret with her gifts of composition and performance. She has sung her original Christian songs in services and they have been a blessing to the Church. Our worship has been enhanced by her contributions. More recently Margaret has begun discerning God's promptings in scripture and then she has created blogs and reflections to encourage people to faith and in developing their faith. These reflections are really good. Spurred on by the touch of His Spirit Margaret unfurls the importance of centuries old scripture for today's world and God truly does speak through her words.

Do not miss out. Find a quiet corner and savour this book. Come into His presence and be prepared to be blessed.

Revd Canon Nigel Washington

September 2022

ACKOWLEDGEMENTS

I would like to acknowledge the support of a number of people in this project:

My heartfelt thanks go to:

- Robert, my husband for allowing me the use of our best computer to work on and the almost exclusive use of our office room
- David, my son for helping me to set up the blog
- Abby, Esther, Hannah and David my children for supporting me in the initial recording and performing of my songs in church. This was the start of sharing my faith through music and writing
- Revd. Canon Nigel Washington, my Vicar, who encouraged me to develop my gifting and share songs in church services
- Jon Denman, who has diligently and patiently proof-read my reflections for this book
- Vicky Yorke, who has supported with proof-reading and page layout
- Chris Malone, who recorded my songs so professionally to enable me to produce a CD

Thank you all for your contributions and encouragement, without which this book would never have been produced.

CONTENTS

Reflections

                                          Page

1. THE GREATEST INVITATION 1
2. LOST AND FOUND 5
3. THE GREAT BANQUET 7
4. YOUR FAMILY'S DESTINY 11
5. BOWLS IN HEAVEN 14
6. GOD'S GARDEN 16
7, THE GOOD STEWARD 22
8. SHOES FIT FOR PURPOSE 29
9. LIVING IN GOD'S REST 34
10. BREAKFAST WITH JESUS 40
11. THE MAZE OF CONFUSION 43
12. A TREE PLANTED BY THE WATERSIDE ... 47

1. THE GREATEST INVITATION

'Behold, I stand at the door and knock. If anyone hears my voice, and opens the door I will come in and eat with him and he with me.'
Revelation 3:20

Everyone likes to receive an invitation. There is something very special about being invited to someone's home or to a special event. It means that person values you and wants to spend time in your company for a period of time, maybe a few hours, a day, a week, or even more. I wonder what invitations you have received and which of these have meant the most to you? On my office wall is a picture which always stirs my heart. It is called 'Jesus, the Light of the World ' by William Holman-Hunt. It depicts Jesus, holding a lantern, standing outside a wooden door, knocking. The door is surrounded by brambles and weeds and has a neglected feel about it. Indeed, one might wonder if anyone is living there at all. Yet Jesus is patiently standing, waiting and knocking. How long has He been there? Will there be a response? How long will He wait and what will be the outcome?

While contemplating this I recall how as a child I used to accompany my mum when she collected money for a charity known as the Mission to Deep Sea Fishermen. This involved delivering envelopes to houses in the local area and then calling to collect them, hopefully containing donations, a few days later. It fascinated me to observe the varying responses from the different people. Some would answer but be abrupt in their response, even rude, while others would not answer at all, leaving us standing uncertainly for several minutes before turning away. The most pleasant responses were when the door was opened wide and we were greeted with a warm smile and an envelope containing a prepared donation. The person might wish us well and we would go on our way feeling blessed and encouraged. Remembering these experiences of waiting for the door to be opened I can sense the longing in Jesus' heart as he waits.

As I look at Jesus knocking on the door, I wonder who is on the other side and how will they choose to respond. Will they ignore His knock altogether, will they take a long time to answer, coming to the door slowly and reluctantly, maybe with fear and suspicion? Will their response be rude and abusive, ending with an outright rejection, or will it be one of warmth, welcome and joyful acceptance?

Jesus promised that to those who open the door of their hearts and receive Him as saviour and Lord there will be abundant life, both now and for eternity. He said *'I will come in and eat with him and he with me.'* This is His invitation to us; an invitation that carries with it a promise so amazing it is life changing!

If *anyone* responds to Jesus knocking on their heart's door and welcomes Him in He will come in and be with them. To think that He loves us that much, and when He resides in us, He will make all things new. But there is a handle only on one side of the door. He will not force His way in. We have to actively open the door and receive Him. Our response to His invitation must be to offer an invitation in return – an invitation to Him to come in.

Inside there is probably dust, dirt, mess and clutter, representing the wrong doing, mistakes, fears, and confusion which cause the lack of peace in the lives of those who have not received Jesus. Many people feel that they have to get their mess sorted out and clean up their act before they can ask Jesus in, but He accepts us as we are. No one is worthy, yet from the moment we invite Him in, His presence is with us. As we spend time with Him, talking and sharing with Him, He works in us and changes us – it becomes a partnership rather than us striving alone to get everything right.

What a change He makes! He brings grace, forgiveness and an assurance of eternity with Him. He gives a promise that He will always be with us, loves us unconditionally and He is a perfect Father. He gives purpose to our lives – and courage to pursue that purpose.

He brings hope, even in the darkest times. Nicky Gumbel, former vicar of large central London church, in a commentary in The Bible in One Year says, *'As we have studied the entire Bible throughout the year, we have seen that we should not expect an easy life. The Bible is true to real life. Life involves many struggles, trials, tests, temptations, difficulties and battles. Yet, in Christ you can be an overcomer, through God's love '*.

I have some dear friends who have gone through and are currently going through struggles, challenges, traumas and disappointments of many kinds; loss, bereavement, unemployment, debilitating health issues, rejection, relationship breakdown and more, yet each one has testified to the transforming presence of Jesus in their lives, giving strength, comfort and hope.

As I was thinking about the picture, I asked the Lord how he feels when his knock is not answered. The sense I had was that He was saying, 'I feel like you do when one of your children is lost or has left home, does not contact you and shows no interest in maintaining a relationship with you. The hurt and disappointment you feel when you eagerly watch and hope but there is no response is what I experience too. Yet I never give up knocking and waiting, in the hope that one day they will welcome me in.

How will you respond to Jesus' knock?

Invite Him in today

If you have never opened the door of your heart and asked Jesus to come into your life, I invite you to do so now by praying a simple prayer:

Prayer
Dear Lord Jesus, Thank you that you came into the world to die for me. Thank you that you are patiently standing, knocking on the door of my heart. Today I choose to open the door and invite you in. Please come into my life and have fellowship with me. Please forgive my wrong doing and clean up the mess and clutter I have created. Let your love fill me and change my life. Amen.

I feel it is important to add that once Jesus is invited in, we should not leave Him standing in the hallway but allow Him into every room, so our hearts become His home. Just let His love fill our hearts more and more so we are transformed. I trust that all who receive Him will experience love, peace, hope and joy as they grow in their relationship with Him. May God bless you as you love and serve Jesus, our Saviour.

2. LOST AND FOUND

Then Jesus told them this parable: "Suppose one of you has a hundred sheep and loses one of them. Doesn't he leave the ninety-nine in the open country and go after the lost sheep until he finds it? And when he finds it, he joyfully puts it on his shoulders and goes home. Then he calls his friends and neighbours together and says, 'Rejoice with me; I have found my lost sheep.' I tell you that in the same way there will be more rejoicing in heaven over one sinner who repents than over ninety-nine righteous persons who do not need to repent."

Matthew 18:10-14

Have you lost anything of great value, or something very precious to you? The sense of relief you feel when you find it again is immense. But worse, have you ever lost a child? I recall one occasion when my son was about fifteen years of age he was lost, after a football match. I couldn't find him anywhere and no one had seen him leave. I made phone calls, and drove all around the area to look in different places where he could be. I still remember the panic I felt when after an hour I still hadn't found him. When I did eventually find him standing in an alleyway just outside the field, my relief cannot be described!

As I reflected on this experience God gave me a picture of a father searching for His children in a thick forest. He would not give up searching until each one was found. Then I saw a river flowing in all directions, through streets, alleyways, buildings, fields, valleys, towns. Over it all stood the cross. The river represented the love of God flowing full and free, compelling, irresistible and overwhelming.

If you are already a believer, then pray that you would be able to do your part in spreading the message of His love. Let us all ask God to show us what our unique assignment is to bring His love and truth to our hurting world.

If you do not yet know God, then let the river of His love carry you along. Don't try to resist it; be caught up in His love and embrace it.

Father God is longing to find you, His precious child. He is desperate for all His lost children to come to Him, not remain separated. He is searching constantly and calling your name, to come to Him and be safe with Him.

The Bible is really one long story about how God our Father is searching for His lost children. Won't you respond to His call today and run into His loving arms? How amazing it is to be totally overwhelmed by His love as He welcomes and accepts us as we are, unconditionally. We can accept and receive this amazing love through the sacrifice of Jesus Christ upon the cross.

There will be a huge celebration in heaven when you are found!

See what great love the Father has lavished on us, that we should be called the children of God! And that is what we are! 1 John 3:1

Prayer
Loving Father, I thank you that you love me so much and you search for me until I am found, calling my name. I choose to come to you now and to be safe in your arms. Thank you that you died for me. Help me to share this wonderful news with others, so that they too may know you and your amazing love. Amen

3. THE GREAT BANQUET

When one of those at the table with him said to Jesus, "Blessed is the man who will eat at the feast in the kingdom of God."

Jesus replied: "A certain man was preparing a great banquet and invited many guests. At the time of the banquet he sent his servant to tell those who had been invited, 'Come, for everything is now ready.'

But they all alike began to make excuses. The first said, 'I have just bought a field and I must go and see it. Please excuse me'. Another said, 'I have just bought five yoke of oxen and I'm on my way to try them out. Please excuse me.' Still, another said, 'I have just got married, so I can't come.'

The servant came back and reported this to his master. Then the owner of the house became angry and ordered his servant, 'Go out quickly into the streets and alleys of the town and bring in the poor, the crippled, the blind and the lame.'

'Sir,' the servant said, 'what you have ordered has been done, but there is still room.' Then the master told his servant, 'Go out to the roads and the country lanes and make them come in, so that my house will be full. I tell you, not one of those men who were invited will get a taste of my banquet.' Luke 14:15-24

As a mother of three married daughters, I have experienced being part of wedding planning and organisation and I know some of the stresses involved! One of the first things to consider when planning an event is who to invite. This can cause considerable heartache as, with a limited number of places available, difficult decisions have to be made and not everyone in our wider circle of family and friends can be included.

Once guests have been invited, we then have to wait for their replies. Some guests reply very quickly and with a definite answer. This helps enormously in the rest of the planning as we know where we stand and if others can now be included. It is wonderful when someone gladly accepts the invitation and this adds to the excitement and anticipation of the big day. When an invitation is declined, however, it can bring a touch of sadness, though often there are valid reasons why the person cannot come. The most frustrating responses are the 'maybes' and those who do not reply at all until asked again, sometimes right up to the deadline.

In the Parable of the Great Banquet the first group of invited guests make excuses as to why they cannot come. These include business, property and relationships. We know that the master is angry and disappointed at their refusal and he sends his servants out to ask others who were not on his initial list. In fact, he is desperate for people to come, as he orders his servants to go everywhere they can to find people and 'compel' them to come. The master represents Jesus, the Son of God, inviting people to accept His invitation to life with Him now and for eternity made possible by His sacrifice on the cross. The invitation first went out to the Jews, God's chosen people, but they failed to recognise Jesus as their Messiah, so the invitation was extended to include everyone else - that means us too! God longs with a passion that everyone should respond to Jesus' invitation of salvation. He does not want anyone to decline. He is desperately calling to those who do not know Him to make that choice, accept His free invitation to be present at the Banquet and be with Him for eternity. Who would want to say no to such an invitation? It carries a promise of forgiveness from sin, eternal life after death and abundant life here on earth, lived in close relationship with Jesus. Why then, do so many not respond to this amazing invitation from the King of Kings? After all, anyone who receives an invitation from a queen or king is deeply honoured, proud and delighted to accept.

I think that clues may be found when we look at the excuses given in the parable. How easy it is to allow our work, possessions and relationships to become so all-consuming that they become all that matters to us and occupy our minds to the extent that we cannot see beyond them. Yet Jesus tells us to *'Seek the Kingdom of God above all else, and live righteously, and he will give you everything you need.* Matthew 6:33 (New Living Translation) I believe this means that as we surrender our lives to Jesus and get to know and love Him more, we will find that our relationship with Him becomes all important. Our perspective shifts, so things which were important to us become less so as we devote our lives to pleasing Him. In the process we discover that He takes care of every detail of our lives so we do not have to stress about them.

Although I am definitely a 'work in progress' and still have areas of my life where I am not fully surrendered to God, I will try to give an example of a personal challenge I faced when I knew I had to make a choice over a particular issue. The example is similar to another which I have included in a later Reflection - 'Living in God's Rest'.

I enjoyed my job, yet found that working full time was becoming all-consuming of my time and mental energy, leaving little room for prayer, bible study or developing gifts God had given me. I had been writing my own songs for a few years but never had time to devote to working on these in more depth or to find ways of using them to bless others. Friends of mine of a similar age had reduced their working hours and I found the thought of this attractive, believing it would lighten the load and allow more space for me to devote myself to growing the Kingdom of God. After praying about this I felt that God was confirming to me that it was the right way forward. There was a problem, however, reducing my hours would mean less pay. I had always relied on a regular income for security and although I knew in my head that God would provide, I had never had the faith or courage to take Him at His word. The time came when I knew I had to make a decision soon because of the cut- off date for change of contracts.

After prayer and seeking agreement from my husband, I knew that the right choice was to step out in faith and reduce my hours. I know that others have given up far more than this, but for me, at that time, it was the step God was encouraging me to take. Decision made, I approached my boss and received approval that my request could be granted. I thus reduced my hours to four days a week, then two years later to three days, and finally to two days. Never once did I look back. The Lord was faithful and provided for us in every way. Indeed, I really felt that the kingdom of God was 'added to me' after seeking to put God first in this matter.

If you have not yet accepted Jesus' invitation to the Great Banquet, take time today to consider what you have to gain…and lose if you reject it. Making the choice to receive Jesus as your Saviour and Lord is the most important decision you will ever make. My heartfelt prayer is that you will accept it and enter into a new life with the King of Kings. Do not delay!

Prayer
Dear Jesus, I thank you for your invitation to the Great Banquet. I am sorry I have ignored You for so long and regarded other things in my life as being more important. Today I gladly choose to accept your invitation. I give my life to You today and ask You to come in and change me.
Amen

4. YOUR FAMILY'S DESTINY

Individually and collectively designed by the Master

It is delightful to see a vase of flowers, hand - picked, carefully selected and lovingly arranged to create something of beauty, bringing peace, joy and a sense of well-being to those who see it. A lovely touch to any room.

Recently my husband and I celebrated our Ruby Wedding Anniversary. Our children very thoughtfully planned a surprise tea party and presented us with a stunning bouquet as a gift. As I enjoyed the flowers over the next few days, they made me think of a family or group of people. The flowers together complement one another to create a specific presentation, giving an overall effect, yet each flower is unique, a masterpiece and lovely on its own. The designer has purpose in mind and knows just how to arrange them so that none overshadows another, colours blend well or contrast effectively so each flower can be seen to its best advantage.

God is the Master Designer. He planned the gender, character and position of each one in the family. Each member is unique and has a specific purpose which no-one else can fulfil.

However, I also have a sense that the family as a whole has a God-given purpose and destiny; the individual members, like flowers which make up a bouquet, complement one another to make a strong unit which God can use for His purposes.

Choosing names for our children can be exciting but also quite challenging as we consider our preferences and also the meanings. In the Bible, great importance and significance is given to names. There are many instances when an individual is given a name which reflects their God-given destiny. Peter is one example of this, when Jesus says in Matthew 16:18, *"Now I say to you that you are Peter (which means 'rock'), and upon this rock I will build my church, and all the powers of hell will not conquer it."* (New Living Translation). Jacob, in the Old Testament, was renamed Israel, which means 'wrestles with God'. Genesis 32:28 If the names of individuals carry such significance, could it also be that the *family* name bears a similar meaning? That is an interesting thought, but suffice it to say that God's desire is for families to be united in love, supporting one another in serving Him together and encouraging each individual to pursue their unique gifting to fulfil the purpose He has for them.

Points to ponder

Examine your own heart for anything which may be preventing God's love and healing from flowing. Are there hindrances to family unity and love?

- pray for healing of relationships and allow forgiveness to flow between you.

- seek the Lord for what is on His heart for your family

- pray for them to know and love Jesus as their Saviour, teaching and encouraging them in the ways of the Lord

- parents, pray for your children and help them discover their God-given gifts and talents. Do all you can to nurture and encourage them

- pray that the God-given destiny of the family as a whole and individually will be fulfilled so that God may be glorified

Prayer
Dear Heavenly Father
Thank you for placing me in a family and for each member of that family. I offer each one to you, that we may all know You and fulfil the plans and purposes you have for us. May our family bring You joy and delight as we love and serve you individually and together. In Jesus' name, Amen

5. BOWLS IN HEAVEN
Every Prayer Counts

One morning, at the beginning of the Coronavirus pandemic, I had to go to the local Co-op to buy some potatoes and, due to the social distancing procedures, had to queue for some time outside the shop. The queue had about twenty people in it and I was about 6th in line. Whenever someone came out another was allowed in. As slowly the queue started to move forward a few steps at a time a song came into my mind- *'We want to see Jesus lifted high'* by Doug Horley, particularly the line:

'Step by step we're moving forward, little by little taking ground'

I thought this a bit amusing, and it helped to relieve the boredom of waiting, but then the next lines came to mind:

'Every prayer a powerful weapon
Strongholds come tumbling down and down and down and down'

Through these words the Lord reminded me of the need to keep praying for family and friends who do not know Him yet. Is there someone for whom you have been praying for a long time and seen no apparent progress? Maybe you think it is pointless and nothing is happening. I know I think this way at times. But take heart! **Every** prayer is a powerful weapon, each prayer counts and gradually the enemy's hold is being weakened. If God has put it into your heart to pray for a person or situation and you are in agreement with Him then together you and God are unbeatable. Remember, the prayers of the saints are filling those bowls in heaven and are a sweet- smelling fragrance to the Lord:

Another angel, who had a golden censer, came and stood at the altar. He was given much incense to offer, with the prayers of all the saints, on the golden altar before the throne. The smoke of the incense, together with the prayers of the saints, went up before God from the angel's hand. Revelation 8:3-5

He is working even though we can't see or feel it. And much activity is taking place in the spiritual realm because of your prayers Don't give up!

Let us not become weary in doing good, for at the proper time we will reap a harvest if we do not give up. Galatians 6:9

Prayer

Heavenly Father, Thank you that every sincere prayer makes a difference and is a powerful spiritual weapon. Please help me not to grow tired and give up but to persistently pray for those people and situations that You have placed on my heart. May my heart be aligned with Yours so that I pray in agreement with You. When I feel discouraged give me a fresh revelation to spur me on in the spiritual battle until I see victory. In Jesus' name. Amen

6. GOD'S GARDEN

'In that day- "Sing about a fruitful vineyard; I, the Lord, watch over it; I water it continually. I guard it day and night so that no-one may harm it." Isaiah 27:2,3

I love the idea that God tends His vineyard and cares for it scrupulously and continually. Although few of us will own a vineyard, it is likely that we will have a garden or have enjoyed a garden at some time and it is from the perspective of tending a garden that I would like to explore this theme.

Although I grew up with a large garden and spent many happy hours playing there as a child, and had parents who enjoyed growing their own fruit and vegetables, my own family have never been keen gardeners. In fact, I am sorry to have to admit that for years the best we could manage was to mow the lawn when it got too unsightly and maybe pull out a few weeds here and there. We did buy and plant a few items such as rose bushes and an apple tree, but generally any natural beauty that existed happened by chance rather than planning or good maintenance! Being a full-time teacher and having four children also meant that time and energy for gardening was limited. I would often admire other peoples' gardens and sometimes felt ashamed of my own, wishing that I had the creative gift of designing and making it well laid out and attractive.

When I became semi-retired in 2018, with the encouragement and help of one of my daughters I started to work on different areas in the house to de-clutter and re-organise space and get some much - needed decorating and home improvement done. This was satisfying and the next task to consider was the garden, although I did not really have much idea of what I wanted or where to start. It was a very pleasant surprise, therefore, when my son, who had just finished his university course, began to show an interest in developing the garden. He and I visited garden centres together and little by little the garden began to take shape as he created attractive areas using wooden edging, planters and rocks to accommodate a variety of plants of assorted colours and shades. Although there is still more to be done it looks so much better than previously and reflects the love, care and hard work that he has put into it.

As I look around at the different aspects of our garden, I often see analogies to illustrate how God works in our lives to bring something beautiful from us, in the same way that we work hard to create a place of beauty which will bring us pleasure. Indeed, a keen gardener will know exactly where they have put each plant and will have carefully considered the best place for it, whether it should be in the sun or the shade, the type of soil needed for it to thrive, the size of pot or planter that is best suited to it, the amount of space it will need and where it will look best in relation to other features of the garden. If we can show love and care for our plants how much more will God, the master gardener, care for us.

He 'plants' us in the right soil

He ensures we are in the best environment to grow and thrive so that we bear fruit, giving pleasure to those around us. He gives us opportunities to reach our potential by bringing people and situations into our lives that will bless and encourage us, sometimes stretching and challenging us.

In my own experience I can look back over the years and see how He has brought others alongside me at different times whose friendship, experience and gentle encouragement have helped to build my faith or develop my giftings.

One such example is at a time when I was not attending church and did not have any Christian friends to support me. My mother had been praying specifically that I would find a church to attend.

One day, when returning home on the bus from a shopping trip, my husband and I met a couple whom my husband had known many years previously at school. They told us about a small Christian fellowship that they attended and how a pianist was needed to lead the worship. I told them that I could play the piano and they invited us to go the following Sunday. We accepted the invitation and were very quickly welcomed into the fellowship where we attended for a number of years and made some good friends who were a blessing and encouragement at a time when we needed it. It also developed my skills in providing a lead in worship and made a way for me to grow closer to the Lord through song and music, things which He undoubtedly wanted to use in the future.

In more recent years I can see how He has blessed me with many good friends and close relationships which have provided amazing support as we have prayed together and spoken into each other's lives often through times of great challenge and difficulty. One of these ladies had experienced many difficulties and disappointments in her life and a few years ago moved house and lived in the same cul-de-sac as me, on the opposite side of the road! God used this for the benefit of both of us, as we began to share in Christian ministries together, specifically a prayer ministry called Healing Rooms held in a local café.

He values us as individuals

Each individual plant has a unique character with its own shape, height, colour and leaf design, bringing its own qualities and interest to the overall effect. Some flower year after year while others have a much shorter existence.

We have a large number of poppies in our garden, all of which just appeared- we did not plant them. They look beautiful while they are in flower but fade very quickly, literally here today and gone tomorrow. Nevertheless, they have an effect of their own which adds to the character of the garden, even if only for a brief time. I feel the same is true of every human life. God has plans and purposes for every individual ever born and each one has a unique part to play and contribution to make to the world and God's kingdom. Sadly, many lives are overlooked and considered of little worth, but our loving Father treasures each one. *'For we are God's workmanship, created in Christ Jesus to do good works, which God created in advance for us to do.'* Ephesians 2:10

He maintains the soil and keeps it clear

Regular weeding is needed to keep the soil clear to prevent plants being choked. Sometimes certain plants have to be removed because they obscure and crowd out smaller plants. How often does God, unbeknownst to us, remove 'weeds' from our soil - situations or people who would have a detrimental effect on us? However, we too have the responsibility to examine our own lives to see if there are weeds which need pulling out, maybe bad habits or wrong thoughts, or even relationships which are not healthy and which distract us from our relationship with our Father.

On this same theme, sometimes a tree or shrub needs to be removed completely, the roots dug up and the tree destroyed. We had a tree in the corner of our garden whose roots were spreading out across the whole area and were in danger of encroaching on the house foundations. The tree had to be uprooted and removed to prevent damage to our home. In the same way, drastic action sometimes has to be taken in our own lives, roots of bitterness or unforgiveness may need to be pulled up and thrown away before our relationships with God and others are poisoned.

He prunes us for greater fruitfulness

"I am the true vine and my Father is the gardener. He cuts off every branch in me that bears no fruit, while every branch that does bear fruit he prunes so that it will be even more fruitful." John 15:1, 2

By our back wall is an apple tree that we planted when we first moved to our house in the '90s. It produced fruit, but many of the apples would fall off into the road on the other side, because the branches had extended so far out. There were so many apples on the ground outside, many getting squashed and rotten, that a neighbour complained and we had no choice but to cut the tree down. It was cut almost down to its stump, much to our sadness because we loved the tree, and we really did not expect it to grow again. But grow it did, and a year later branches and leaves were sprouting in profusion with the promise that fruit would once again be produced.

God may have to take drastic action in our lives in order to produce greater fruitfulness. This is hard to understand but we are told that *'God disciplines those He loves and He punishes everyone He receives as a son.'* Hebrews 12:6. Although we cannot always see the reason why we have to go through times of testing we have to believe that it is for our good and comes from the hand of a loving Father.

The purpose of a garden is for enjoyment, rest, peace, beauty and fruitfulness. Our purpose as the body of Christ is to work with our

Father, the gardener, and accept His planting and pruning to grow in our faith and in His likeness, in order that we may produce good, healthy and delicious fruit. This will bring joy and fulfilment to us and delight and glory to Him. How wonderful that God is the master gardener. He is not too busy, too tired or too unimaginative to create a beautiful garden in the lives of His children or the collective lives that comprise His Church, the Bride of Christ.

"I am the vine; you are the branches. If a man remains in me and I in him, he will bear much fruit; apart from me you can do nothing."
John 15:5

Prayer
Father, Help me to remain in You, the true Vine, responding to Your loving care and discipline as You perfect me for Your glory. Amen

7. THE GOOD STEWARD
The Parable of the Talents

"Again, it will be like a man going on a journey, who called his servants and entrusted his wealth to them. To one he gave five bags of gold, to another two bags, and to another one bag, each according to his ability. Then he went on his journey. The man who had received five bags of gold went at once and put his money to work and gained five bags more. So also, the one with two bags of gold gained two more. But the man who had received one bag went off, dug a hole in the ground and hid his master's money.

After a long time the master of those servants returned and settled accounts with them. The man who had received five bags of gold brought the other five. 'Master,' he said, 'you entrusted me with five bags of gold. See, I have gained five more.' His master replied, 'Well done, good and faithful servant! You have been faithful with a few things; I will put you in charge of many things. Come and share your master's happiness!' The man with two bags of gold also came. 'Master,' he said, 'you entrusted me with two bags of gold; see, I have gained two more.' His master replied, 'Well done, good and faithful servant! You have been faithful with a few things; I will put you in charge of many things. Come and share your master's happiness!'

Then the man who had received one bag of gold came. 'Master,' he said, 'I knew that you are a hard man, harvesting where you have not sown and gathering where you have not scattered seed. So I was afraid and went out and hid your gold in the ground. See, here is what belongs to you.' His master replied, 'You wicked, lazy servant! So you knew that I harvest where I have not sown and gather where I have not scattered seed? Well then, you should have put my money on deposit with the bankers, so that when I returned I would have received it back with interest.

'So take the bag of gold from him and give it to the one who has ten bags. For whoever has will be given more, and they will have an abundance. Whoever does not have, even what they have will be taken from them. And throw that worthless servant outside, into the darkness, where there will be weeping and gnashing of teeth.'
Matthew 25:14-30

In this parable we read of how three servants are held accountable to their master for the way they use the 'talents' he has entrusted them with. Two of them please the master with the good returns they made with his investment, but the third receives an angry and condemning response because he did nothing with the talent he had been given. Whenever I read this story, I am tempted to feel at best uneasy and at worse, terrified. I'm sure that I am not alone. But this attitude fails to understand what the parable is all about; it does not take into account the loving and forgiving character of Jesus.

To clarify, the **'Master'** clearly represents Jesus. **'The talents'** represent everything that God has given us. In the story, the talents were sums of money but for us I believe they can mean our time, wealth, skills and abilities, interests, characteristics and personal qualities, spiritual insights and revelation. Our whole lives, in fact. There are different interpretations but I would suggest that **the 'first two servants'** who made good returns, represent those who have a relationship with Jesus and try to follow Him. The **'third servant'**, who did nothing with his talent,

"Well done, good and faithful servant."

represents those who may think they are following Jesus but are not committed and do not have a relationship with Him.

The parable is all about using the talents God has given us as he wants us to or, to put it another way, being good stewards of those talents. As we unpack the meaning of this parable, we will consider what our talents are, why we should use our talents, and what might stop us from using them, and how we can use them well, living our lives in a way that is pleasing to the Master.

WHY SHOULD WE USE OUR TALENTS?

When we receive Jesus as Saviour, our lives are no longer ours - they are His – and, although we often fail, we will have a desire to follow Him and use the talents He has given us in the way that pleases Him.

The scriptures make it clear that God knows and loves each one of us and that we are unique individuals with a specific calling on our lives that no-one else can fulfil. Psalm 139, a well-known and well-loved Psalm, says '*My frame was not hidden from you when I was made in the secret place, when I was woven together in the depths of the earth. Your eyes saw my unformed body; all the days ordained for me were written in your book before one of them came to be*'. In Ephesians 2:10 we are told, '*For we are God's workmanship, created in Christ Jesus to do good works, which God prepared in advance for us to do*'.

WHAT ARE OUR TALENTS and how can we recognise them?

Here are some questions to ask ourselves:
What blessings do we have? What has God given us and blessed us with? Do we have a home, food, a job? Do we have Christian fellowship, teaching and resources? Not everyone has these things. Let's be thankful for what we have and ask how we could share them with others and use them for God's kingdom.

What are our responsibilities? Raising a family, managing a home, earning a living, serving in church will all feature largely for most of us. I believe responsibilities and duties can be fulfilled with an attitude of joy and are an important part of serving God and using our talents.

What are we naturally good at? Is it administrating, organising, teaching, practical skills, technology? Whatever it is, it is a gift from God which He wants us to use.

What tasks and activities give us joy? When am I in my element? For some, it might be a creative talent such as gardening, cooking, designing, painting, or music. For others it might be helping and encouraging, serving, visiting or giving practical care and support. Again, God will have put this passion in us and wants us to use it.

As we reflect on these things a picture will emerge of just how much God has blessed us and also the things that make us uniquely the person God created us to be.

I will share a bit of my own story here. One Sunday, about ten years ago, my vicar preached on this parable. I felt the Holy Spirit convinced me that I should use my gift of music and song writing to extend the kingdom of God. I am naturally quite reserved and do not like being in the spotlight so it was a challenge, but I spoke to the vicar and shared what God had put on my heart. My vicar gave me opportunities to use my songs and music in church and I began to place my musical talent in God's hands and allow Him to use it as he desired.

WHAT MIGHT STOP US FROM USING OUR TALENTS?

There are many reasons, I believe, but I think most will fall into one of the following categories:

Fear: The third servant did not know the master; he had no relationship with Him and allowed fear to direct his actions. Fear of failure resulted in him making no effort and therefore producing nothing. Could it be that we too do not use our talents because we are fearful? Perhaps we are afraid of failure or rejection, or of not being as good as others. But the Bible tells us: *'There is no fear in love, for perfect love casts out fear, because fear has to do with punishment. The one who fears is not made perfect in love.'* 1 John 4:18

Sometimes, fear may stem from condemning or critical words spoken over us in the past, words such as ''you're useless, you'll never amount to anything''. We may have been harshly criticised or punished for making mistakes, resulting in damaged confidence and a crushed spirit. In order to protect ourselves from further hurt we may play it safe and not do anything which takes us out of our comfort zone. If we have been crushed in this way, there is healing available through the Holy Spirit.

Low Self-Worth - I have nothing worthwhile to offer: You may feel you can't do anything particularly well. Or poor health and limited capacity may restrict what you are able to do. But I believe everyone, no matter what their situation, can do something. My dad, in his later years lived in a care home, and although he couldn't go out due to his poor mobility, he chose to devote time each day in praying faithfully for his family, the Church, the nation, and the carers and patients in the home. He also befriended another elderly resident, praying with her every day and talking to her about Jesus. He really let his light shine.

Time Pressure: Being over-pressurised and too busy is a very common reason for not using our talents to the full. Do you ever feel that your life is so busy that you are trying to keep dozens of plates spinning? The question to ask in this situation is; why am I doing what I do? Does God actually want me to do all these things, or am I doing them for the wrong reason? We saw earlier that we have a unique role to play and purpose to fulfil. If we are too busy then we may miss the thing God has <u>really</u> called us to do. This topic is a whole subject in itself, as I explore in my Reflection 'Living in God's Rest,' but if we are over – pressurised, over- stressed and over- committed then we should stop and take a good long look at what makes us so busy and ask the Holy Spirit to show us which of these tasks and activities He wants us to continue and which we should put to one side or stop. This is an area in which I struggle and I am working through it with the Holy Spirit, to attain the peace and freedom He wants me to enjoy.

HOW CAN WE BE GOOD STEWARDS? What is the solution?

The good news is that we do not have to live perfect lives in our own strength! Although we may struggle and fail many times, God gives us grace, mercy and help along the way. Despite all the obstacles we looked at, *there is hope*! The Holy Spirit is there to help us all the time. If we ask Him, He will show us how we should be using our talents and how to do this without striving and being over busy. We can and should repent of failure to be good stewards and with the Holy Spirit's help devote ourselves wholeheartedly to running the race He has set before us.

The most fundamental thing, I believe, is that we have a *close personal relationship* with Jesus. From an intimate relationship will flow love and trust and it is from this that our good works should come. Everything we do should come from a heart of love and a desire to serve Him, rather than from a sense of duty or fear of punishment. The things we do for Him should be a joy, not a drudgery. If we do not have this joy, we should ask Him why and receive the healing that He offers. If we spend time with Him, we will know His heart. He will put *His* desires into our heart so they become *our* desires! So, if you have a desire to visit the sick or lonely people, help the homeless, write poetry or arrange flowers, God will have given you this desire.

God has set us up for success

The Lord knows our potential and abilities and will not ask us to do anything He has not equipped us for. The three servants were not all given the same amount, so this suggests that the master had different expectations for each of them. The third servant failed because he had no relationship with the master. But we have been given every opportunity to enter into relationship with our Master through His sacrifice on the cross and His resurrection. The way is open for us. Let us choose to spend time in His presence and experience His love and grace as He helps us on the journey. Let us find the joy and peace that is available to us when we surrender to Him and gladly become partners with Him in extending the Kingdom of God. No matter what our weaknesses and failings are, or how old we are, it is never too late! He has set us up for success! I want to focus on the race God has set before me and not be distracted. I want Him to say to me, "Well done, good and faithful servant!" I pray that this will be true for all of us.

May we receive heavenly rewards for being good stewards of our talents.

Prayer
Father God, Thank you that you know me intimately, you love me and have made me a unique individual with a special set of skills and talents. I surrender all that I am and have to you and ask that you will help me to use my God-given talents for your glory and complete the particular tasks that you have given me to do. I reject fear and believe that your Holy Spirit will guide and equip me as I step out in obedience to you. Thank you, Father. Amen

8. SHOES FIT FOR PURPOSE

He makes my feet like the feet of a deer; ...he enables me to stand on the heights. Psalm 18:33

This passage was one of my daily readings recently. After reading it, I prayed that God would lead and guide me along the path He has chosen for me, giving me the strength and ability to be faithful in the tasks He has entrusted me with and enabling me to reach the 'heights' necessary to fulfil my God-given destiny.

Pausing, I asked Him if there was anything He wanted to say or show me in response to my request. Expecting something warm and encouraging in response, I was a little taken aback to have an image in my mind of Jesus holding out a pair of muddy, tatty old shoes to me, with a look of impatience as He turned as if to walk away.

Time to change

I recognised the shoes as my favourite casual canvas shoes, very old and comfortable, which I use for walking locally. A little hesitantly I asked, 'Lord, they're my own old shoes.... what are you saying to me?' As I waited and listened, I sensed that He was showing me that these shoes, although comfy and familiar, had to be replaced with stronger, more weather-proof ones if I wanted to be properly equipped for the journey ahead. If I was to scale heights and travel along difficult terrain, I must be prepared to let Him show me changes that had to be made in my thinking and attitudes.

He was holding out my comfortable old shoes

Overcoming fear

In my spirit I knew that fear was something I needed to overcome in many areas, particularly in relation to being afraid to confront or speak truth if it might 'rock the boat' or cause people to feel uncomfortable. Specifically, it was being afraid to share the gospel for fear of what people might think. 'Lord', I said, 'I'm sorry. Please help me to overcome my fears and have courage. I really want to travel with You and fulfil my destiny. I don't want to miss out in any way because of fear. Please give me the right shoes.' In reply, I sensed Him smile and say, 'Good. Come on then. There is much to do and time is short.'

Forgiveness

After further prayer and waiting on Him I realised that there were people I needed to forgive, including myself, from past hurts and situations. I also needed to reject the lie that I am insignificant and have nothing worthwhile to offer and that nothing I do or say will make any difference. The Lord also showed me that I needed to confess and ask forgiveness from Him and the people I had hurt in my behaviour towards them. This was challenging but with God's help I was able to do it and the result was a sense of freedom and release. I know there is more to do, and I trust God to bring about opportunities in His timing for these conversations, believing He will give me the grace, humility and courage I will need to be obedient.

Dependence on God for strength

Since then, I have found that I have become a little bolder. I was given the courage to give out pamphlets explaining the gospel message and speak with greater confidence and authority, hearing God's voice more clearly. So, I believe the change has begun, albeit with small steps. But I believe we must really *want* to break through and not settle for staying in our comfort zones. It is imperative that we depend totally on God for our strength, as it is all too easy to slip back into independent mode. *For God did not give us a spirit of timidity or cowardice or fear, but [He has given us a spirit] of power and of love and of sound judgement and personal discipline [abilities that result in a calm, well-balanced mind and self-control].* 2 Timothy 1:7 (Amplified Bible)

The wonderful truth that, as children of God, we are no longer slaves to fear is beautifully expressed in the song *'No Longer Slaves'* by Tasha Cobbs Leonard. In our ongoing battle we need to renew our minds by believing and declaring this truth, knowing in our spirit that '…*the One who is in us is greater than the one who is in the world.'* 1 John 4:4

Intimacy is the key

The key, I believe, is to stay in close relationship with Him, spending time with Him in the 'secret place' of prayer. If we make this a priority in our lives and share our thoughts with Him, we will as well learn to hear the plans He has for us. Through this intimacy will come revelation as He shines His light in every corner of our hearts, showing us areas where He needs to work and steps of obedience we need to take. It may be uncomfortable but He is totally for us, and as we learn to yield to Him, we will experience deeper peace, hope and joy as we walk forward into the destiny He has planned for us.

Intimacy with God in the secret place of prayer

The way ahead

If, like me, you desire to 'scale the heights' and fulfil the destiny God has planned for you, then I encourage you to spend time in that 'secret place'. Just as He revealed to me the steps I needed to take – overcoming fear, forgiving others, repenting of wrong attitudes and mindsets and rejecting the enemy's lies – so He will also highlight to you the areas in your life which He wants to deal with. It is so wonderful to know that He is on our side and is ready and waiting to help us! May God bless you in your journey with Him and may He provide you with shoes fit for the purpose.

Prayer
Heavenly Father, Thank you that You equip me with everything I need to walk the path You have prepared for me. Please help me to renew my mind and to take hold of the truth that you are for me. I want to fulfil the plans and purposes You have for me and not to be constrained by fear but to go forward in faith and confidence that You are with me. Amen

9. LIVING IN GOD'S REST
Are you trying to keep too many plates spinning?

Jesus said, "Come unto me all you who are weary and burdened and I will give you rest.

Take my yoke upon you and learn from me, for I am gentle and humble in heart, and you will rest for your souls. For my yoke is easy and my burden is light." Matthew 11:28-30

There may be things which we long to do to fulfil our desire to honour God by serving Him, but somehow the busy-ness of our life with its many pressures crowds in and we feel we are just surviving rather than truly living. Doing all the right things and ticking all the boxes can be exhausting, like keeping dozens of plates spinning or trying to juggle dozens of balls without dropping one, while in our heart we know that it is impossible to do everything right all the time. Yet Jesus said we can find rest. So how can we find this rest and remain in it?

Let us look at the four main parts of Jesus' invitation in Matthew 11:28-30.

1. Come unto me, all you who are weary and burdened

Take Him at His word and come to Him. Tell Him honestly how you are feeling, what your frustrations are, what you find difficult and ask for His help. Sit quietly and let Him speak to you. Focus your mind on Him.

It is important, I feel, to take an honest look at how we spend our time and energy, evaluating our motives for doing what we do. It might be helpful to make a list of all tasks or activities that occupy our time on a regular basis, asking the Holy Spirit to show us the true motives behind each one, then sort them into categories:

- **Essential Activities:** Which of them are things that are essential, such as caring for home and family, or work commitments?

- **Should or Ought:** Which are the things that we do because we feel we *ought* to do, but may not be called to do? Are there some that we do to impress or win approval from others, including God? Are we performance orientated, always feeling we have to tick all the boxes?

- **Activities for Self-Protection:** Do we keep busy in order to fill a void in our lives, or because we need to be needed? Maybe we want to avoid being alone with our thoughts. Maybe we think we have to hold everything together so we have no choice but to keep everything going, or our world may fall apart.

Which of these situations drain us or leave us feeling unfulfilled?

- **Things We *Want* to Do:** How many of the things we do give real joy and peace? How much time is spent actually doing things we love because we know that is what we were born to do?

- **Things We are *Called* to Do:** Which activities do we feel are a genuine calling from God? There may be activities we are called to do that initially we do not want to do but when we respond to God's call, we find unexpected joy and fulfilment.

Now let us look at the 'should' or 'ought' and the activities for self-protection and ask the Holy Spirit to reveal the reasons behind why we feel the need to be over-busy.

If we ask in sincerity and from a genuine desire to honour Him, He will make it clear if He requires us to continue with all the things we do, or if there is something we should stop. Is it time to take a different direction, share workloads or take a time of rest? Is there something we *should* be doing but are not, because we are too busy doing things we have *not* been called to do? When we come to Him in trust and surrender, He will show us by His Spirit and give us a sense of what to do or not to do.

2. Take My yoke upon you

A yoke is a piece of equipment which kept two oxen together, working side by side. While often thought of as being cumbersome and restrictive, when the two move in synchronisation with each other it is easy and effective. I believe this is what Jesus meant when He said 'take my yoke upon you and learn from me, for I am gentle and humble of heart'.

When we are close to Him, He will put thoughts and desires into our heart which we know in our spirit are from Him. Sometimes the things we find challenging are things God wants us to persevere with and if this is the case He will equip us and give strength for the task. I feel it is a question of discerning when He is calling us to keep going and trust Him because He is shaping and refining us, and when He is saying it is time to stop. Again, this comes from intimacy and walking closely with Him. Often we do not yoke ourselves to Him but live independently of Him, hearing His words and knowing them in our heads but not in our hearts.

3. For My yoke is easy and My burden is light:

Many Christians I have discussed this with say that they know if a decision is right because they have a sense of peace, whereas they have no peace if their decision is not in line with God's plans and purposes. This discernment is only to be found when we are in that place of intimacy with Jesus and in close relationship with Him. Walking in partnership with Him is a joy. We will have a sense of rightness in our spirit, and even when things are busy there will be a sense of purpose and excitement. This is what we will experience when we take His yoke upon us and the promise will be realised; *My yoke is easy and my burden is light.*

I would like to share an example from my own life:

I have gone through two periods in my life where my employment as a teacher was stressful and difficult. In the first of these, even though I wanted to quit, through prayer and spiritual counsel from Christian friends I felt that God would have me keep going because He was using this as a time of training in my life and strengthening of character.

With His help I persevered and the result was increased skill, greater confidence in my work and a deeper trust and reliance on my Heavenly Father.

The second period of difficulty contained a different lesson and a different outcome. Again, I was finding my work challenging and exhausting but this time God asked me to make a change and demonstrate my trust in Him by surrendering my work to Him. About two thirds of the way through this difficult year I attended a Christian conference where the speaker was teaching on Abraham and the Test he faced of sacrificing his only son, Isaac, in response to God's command. The speaker discerned that God was asking us to lay our 'Isaacs' on the altar and surrender them to God.

The following day, in the presence of two close friends, I laid my job on the altar, offering it to the Lord as a sacrifice and trusting Him to give back whatever He chose, even if that meant not having a job at all. I experienced great peace after doing this. Two days later I spoke to my employer and asked if I could reduce my days, adding that if this was not possible, I would be prepared to hand in my notice, as I was finding my present commitment untenable.

Amazingly, he replied that this might well be possible and a few days later he confirmed that I could work two days a week as another colleague also wanted to reduce her hours and her request fitted *like eating with Him. This is what Jesus thinks is normal fellowship. Fellowship is all about an ongoing relationship with Jesus - as close as Him eating with us."*

The idea of 'eating with Jesus' really attracted me, so I put aside my various Bible study guides, set prayers and normal quiet time routines and simply 'had breakfast with Jesus.' I would eat my cereal then sit back with a cup of coffee and talk to Jesus. I would ask Him what He would like to say to me. Then I would listen for His answer, which could come in the form of a thought, a sense or impression, a picture, or a scripture. If there was something causing me concern, I would tell Him about the issue and ask what He would like to say about it. I would write down the conversations and look back over them. After doing this for a few days I began to find it very real and releasing, discovering that I had a greater awareness of His presence with me.

The joy and pleasure of sitting with Jesus is something we need to seek after daily, not only on certain occasions. We need to feed on Him, listen to Him and hear His words of love and encouragement to us. We need physical food regularly, not only when we need extra help or to get us through a difficult day. It is the same with our spiritual food.

We know how it feels to converse with someone who is always clock-watching or not really listening. Maybe we are guilty of this ourselves.

It can be just as frustrating when the other person talks only about themselves without showing interest in or regard for what you are trying to say. I sometimes wonder if Jesus feels this way about my prayers.

It is my belief that Jesus wants us to savour every moment with Him, digesting every word He speaks. He wants us to commune with Him as a friend, sometimes speaking but also listening. He does not want us to rush in with a list of requests, but to simply be with Him, sharing our hearts and letting Him share His.

I have found that this gives me freedom from the 'have-tos' – *I must pray those set prayers, do that devotional, read those prescribed Bible passages, etc.* Although I use these prepared materials regularly and find them useful, I am discovering that just 'eating with Jesus' has brought a fresh life to my quiet times. I can really tune in to Him and what He has to say to me at the start of the day and I then sense His presence with me throughout the remainder of the day.

Hopefully my experience might open up a different and deeper way of praying than simply listing requests with eyes closed and hands together; while there is nothing wrong with that there can be much more to conversing with our saviour and friend.

Let me encourage you to spend quality time with Him.

Eat breakfast with Jesus.

Prayer
Dear Jesus, Thank you that you want to be with me and spend time with me. Thank you that you want to share in every aspect of my life. Please let my times with you be simple, peaceful, meaningful and full of joy.   Amen

11. A MAZE OF CONFUSION

God is our refuge and strength, an ever-present help in trouble. Therefore, we will not fear, though the earth give way, and the mountains fall into the heart of the sea....
He says, "Be still, and know that I am God: I will be exalted among the heathen, I will be exalted in the earth". Psalm 46:1, 2 and 10

At the time of the Coronavirus outbreak in 2019 and the months following there were many prophecies and thoughts expressed about what was happening in the spiritual realm and what it meant for the nations of the world. These included the following opinions:

- it was attack from the Enemy, Satan, and we, the Church, should battle against it in prayer

- the Church was being called to account – it was time to repent, wake up and stop teaching only what people want to hear at the expense of Biblical truth

- we were in the End Times and this was a warning that we should be ready for the return of Jesus to this earth. Darker times were ahead

- it was a judgement from God – punishment for turning away from Him as a nation and denying our need for Him

- although undoubtedly evil, God was allowing this crisis and using it as a means of bringing people to Him

- a huge spiritual harvest and revival were on the way and the Church must be ready to disciple new converts

Nearly three years later in August 2022 we have come out of the pandemic crisis; however, more alarming situations have arisen, namely the invasion of Ukraine by Russia, constant threat of war, climate change bringing extreme weather conditions, previously unknown in this country, bringing drought and potential food shortages. With the unfolding emergency of a cost-of-living crisis things seem to be increasingly spiralling out of control, causing many of us to feel anxious and fearful of the future, both for ourselves and our families.

The prophecies, thoughts and opinions outlined earlier regarding the Coronavirus pandemic can still be applied in the ongoing chaotic state of world and national situations.

While these varying messages can be confusing and even overwhelming, I feel that there is truth in all the above, but let us remember that all prophecy is **only in part.** The news and media focus only on what we see happening in the natural world, whereas prophesy is from the spiritual realm which the natural mind cannot understand.

What should our attitude be?

- stay close to the Lord and focus on Him
- remain in close fellowship with other believers in Jesus, supporting and encouraging one another
- hear and discern what God is calling **you** to do and focus on that wholeheartedly

- love others and share the good news of Jesus at every opportunity
- be mindful of prophecies but test them and do not make them into a doctrine
- be aware of what is going on and what the Enemy is doing but don't make it your focus
- do not live in fear but receive strength and peace from the Lord

The Labyrinth

While thinking about this an image came to mind of a labyrinth, an underground maze of dark, twisting tunnels. It was as though I was walking along these dark, confusing tunnels with no idea of which direction I was heading in or how to get out. Yet I was holding onto a golden thread which guided me along the right path, and at each turn or fork I was following the direction of the thread. The thread was all I had to give me any hope of coming out into the light. This is a powerful analogy, I believe, of the darkness and confusion there is in our world currently, but trusting in God, His Word, the Bible, and a close relationship with Him, is the 'golden thread' which leads us to safety.

Your ears will hear a word behind you,, "This is the way walk in it," whenever you turn to the right or to the left. Isaiah 30:21 (New Living Translation)

Keep believing, keep hoping, keep trusting, keep praying, keep listening. Hold tightly to the golden thread.

Prayer
Dear Father God, Life can be frightening and confusing when things are out of my control. I often don't know what to believe or what to do. I thank you that you are in control and that you never change. Help me to believe your Word and to trust in you no matter what is going on in the world around me. Help me to hold tightly to the truth and trust you to lead me along the right path. Amen

12. A TREE PLANTED BY THE WATERSIDE

Blessed is the man who does not walk in the counsel of the wicked or stand in the way of sinners, or sit in the seat of mockers. But his delight is in the law of the Lord, and on His law he meditates day and night. He is like a tree planted by streams of water, which yields its fruit in season and whose leaf does not wither. Whatever he does prospers.
                                                                Psalm 1:1-3

We have just experienced the driest Spring and Summer in England for many years. In fact, on some days, temperatures have exceeded 40 degrees, which is unprecedented in this country. As a result, grass once green and lush is now an orangey brown and many ponds and streams have dried up. When I took my grandchildren to a local park it was unrecognizable as the beautiful place it once was, with dry earth and dead grass instead of the usual green grassy slopes.

Our local 'dew pond', which a few months ago had been full of water with ducks swimming there, is now completely empty, with only dry, cracked earth and no ducks. We are officially experiencing drought, and there is concern about the future, with regard to food production and water shortages. Many are living in fear of our natural resources running out, which we have taken for granted.

A few days ago, we had a day of heavy rain, and it was so refreshing and uplifting to see areas beginning to show green grass again. It reminded me of how dependent we are upon God for life-giving water. Psalm 1 tells us that those who set their hearts and minds on God, and who delight in Him, are resourced by the living water which flows from the heart of God. A constant supply of blessing which never runs dry, enabling us to stay fresh and green

What are these blessings which come to the 'righteous person'?

Stability

'Our leaves do not wither'. The leaves remain fresh and green, even in drought conditions. When trials and pressures come, although we may still be affected, we have hope, strength, peace and God-given wisdom. We will not collapse under the strain.

A close friend of mine, who is suffering from Motor Neuron Disease, is a living testimony of this. Now living in a Nursing Home, despite her weakening physical condition she is at peace in her spirit, trusting God for the strength she needs each day. Rather than becoming consumed by fear she is resting in God's love and moreover is sharing her faith with other residents by holding a weekly 'Songs of Praise' meeting.

Prosperity

'Whatever he does prospers'. This, I believe, means that if we are aligned with the Will of God, everything we do will come from our relationship with Him, in which we find joy and fulfilment. Our lives will be purposeful and productive. We will be able to maintain focus and clear vision even when there is confusion and fear in the world around us. Psalm 37 expresses it like this: *'The blameless spend their days under the LORD's care and their inheritance will endure forever. In times of disaster they will not wither, in days of famine they will enjoy plenty* Psalm 37:18 &19

Our needs will always be met, sometimes supernaturally, because we stay close to the Lord and listen to Him. I believe this also includes protection. Some friends of mine who travel to various places in the UK preaching, teaching and ministering, are a real example of this. They describe how, on one occasion they were due to travel to Bedfordshire to lead a Bible Study but severe weather conditions meant that motorists were advised not to travel unless essential. There was a hurricane forecast. They prayed and asked the Lord to show them if they should cancel the meeting, but sensed He was telling them to travel as planned and to depend on Him for their safety. They made the journey unscathed, and shared later that debris was being blown all around their car, but not one object actually touched them. They declared that the safest place to be is in the Will of God.

Fruitfulness

'He is like a tree planted by the water which yields its fruit in season'. As righteous people we will show kindness and generosity to others,

giving help and encouragement to those who need it. A true example of this is of a dear friend, who has now passed away, who never failed to have time to listen to those with problems and needs and whose gift of hospitality meant that not a week went by without her welcoming folks into her home, whether to offer a listening ear, counsel or comfort to friends going through challenges and provide a meal for those in need of friendship and support. She would also welcome newcomers into the area and look after neighbour's children

We will hold fast to God's Word and live by it, demonstrating honour and trustworthiness, truth and wisdom in every situation, acting with integrity. Our outworking of the love of God will provide a safe place to which others are drawn.

How can we achieve this? How do we 'delight in the Lord'?

Once we have accepted The Lord into our lives as Saviour, we need to develop our relationship with Him, nurture it and allow it to grow. The phrase 'dwell in His presence' is often used, or 'being in the secret place' with Him. This requires commitment and many of us find it difficult, but I feel it is like knowing Him as a friend, while maintaining an awareness of His awesomeness, power and holiness. Psalm 25: *14* says *'The Lord confides in those who fear Him; he makes His covenant known to them.* How amazing that the Creator of the universe loves us as individuals and desires our friendship!

We will bear fruit even through difficult times

It is about placing Him at the centre of our lives and allowing everything we do to flow from our relationship with Him. I have expressed this in varying ways through the Reflections in this book but in summary I believe the necessary disciplines include the following:

- praise and worship God for who He is acknowledging His greatness, holiness, majesty and power
- give thanks for His love and provision
- read and meditate on the Bible, so it will shape our thoughts, words and actions
- be honest with Him about our struggles and fears and bring all our needs to Him in prayer knowing He is faithful
- trust Him in every situation and listen for His response,
- keep short accounts with God, seeking forgiveness and forgiving those who have hurt us
- be ready to obey Him at all times
- keep in mind that we are in a spiritual battle with an enemy who wants to discourage us to the point of giving up
- put on our 'spiritual armour' as Paul says in Ephesians 6:11-18, and stand firm on the truth that God has given us victory through Christ Jesus
- stay focused, always remembering that God has set us a unique path
- be encouraged to run the race with patience and endurance, our goal being to complete the course and enter into the presence of Jesus to receive our heavenly reward. Hebrews 12:1

If this seems like a tall order, or an impossible task, take heart! To reiterate the message in Reflection 7, *'The Good Steward'* we are not expected to do it on our own...that *is* impossible. God is for, not against us. He is patient, loving and understanding. His Spirit is in us to help, guide, strengthen and encourage us. And Jesus is waiting at the finish line to welcome us.

Praise God! Let me encourage you to keep going on your journey of faith with Him.

This Reflection opened with Psalm 1. Similar thoughts are expressed in Psalm 92, with beautiful imagery, also of trees and plants:

The righteous will flourish like a palm tree, they will grow like a cedar of Lebanon; planted in the house of the Lord, they will flourish in the courts of our God. They will still bear fruit in old age, they will stay fresh and green, proclaiming, 'The Lord is upright, He is my Rock, and there is no wickedness in Him'. Psalm 92:12-15

Prayer

Father God, I praise you for your love, your Word and your faithfulness. I want to be constantly resourced by your living water so I produce good fruit and stay fresh and green. Please help me to remain in your presence and be a living testimony to your goodness. Amen

A BLESSING

The Lord bless you and keep you;
The Lord make His face shine upon you and be gracious to you;
The Lord turn His face towards you and give you peace. Amen.   Numbers 6:22-26

IMAGES

Page	
	Cover Photo, Debby Hudson, Unsplash
1	William Holman Hunt
6	James Wheeler, Unsplash
8	Andra C Taylor, Unsplash
11	Margaret Lim, Author
14	Margaret Lim, Author
16	David Kohler, Unsplash
23	Margaret Lim, Author
28	Selena Gallag, Pixaby
29	Marco Forno , Unsplash
30	Margaret Lim, Author
32	Ben White, Unsplash
34	Margaret Lim, Author
37	Unknown, Unsplash
41	Margaret Lim, Author
45	Bailey Mahon, Unsplash
47	a) Margaret Lim, b) Abby Tebboth
48	Fons Hejnsbroek, Unsplash
50	Margaret Lim, Author
52	Unknown, Unsplash
53	Gabriel Sanchez, Unsplash

https://unsplash.com/images   https://pixabay.com/